# An Atlantic Light

Co Loa Media

# An Atlantic Light

Tony Wailey worked as a seafarer and construction worker for ten years, including periods lost to drugs and teaching English as a Foreign Language. He later studied modern history and wrote a thesis on the Liverpool Seamen. For 25 years he was an advisor to mature students in Universities and Colleges of adult education. He now works as a freelance writer. This is his third collection of poems.

# An Atlantic Light

Tony Wailey

Co Loa Media

First published 2018 by Co Loa Media

Co Loa Media
Cheltenham
GLOS
GL52 2DA

ISBN: 978 0 9928962 7 0

*Designed and typeset by iKraal, Cape Town SA*
*Printed and bound by CPI Group (UK) Ltd, Croydon, CR0 4YY*

For Anna Benedetto

The wash, the plunge
down
        (saying:
we will not become you, we
are the impenitents)
                        the tears.

Robert Creeley
Four Seasons Press
San Francisco, 1969.

'Whenever I think of making a comeback I know I
haven't been drinking enough.'

John Conteh, former world light heavyweight boxing
champion, Radio Merseyside 1985

# CONTENTS

Henrietta 32
Niall 33
Stephanie 34
Flannery 35
'Duke 36
Fiona 37
Phoebe 38
Johnny, George and Alex 39
Eamon 59
Claire 60
Lydia 61
Andrew 62
Nuala 63
Fintan 64
Brigid 65
Cora 66
Dorothea 67
Philip 68
Fallon 69
Briana 70
Isabella 71
Frances 72
Eileen 73
Barbara 74
Bevan 75
Fara 76
Richard 77
Keeva 78
Declan 79
Ardan 80
Dierdre 81
Cody 82
Frederick 83

Liam 84
Joseph 85
Niamh 86
Daniella 87
Sarah 88
Ana 89
Siobahn 90
Billy 91
Robert 92
Susannah 93

## Maeve

I dance like a scarecrow
to make life easy
someone that the wind blows
don't need a path to search
my demand to be free
measure distance lurch
don't worry what I know
thinking only of the sea
it isn't my last moan
I don't do hurt
will never go gently
can you see me in church
even if hopes are torn
put it down to destiny
not the heart with stones
I don't want to be alone
but sometimes honestly
I can't bear the drone
where I want to be.

## Race

Birds can't start their tune
the moon lies in her wake
she asks if I like the blues
sat in bars making bets
she sits there tiny frame
this is how good it gets
like a match stick in ruins
her eyes fill with shame
this is her office room
she doesn't pay rent
it's just a game
she'll live in a tent
a dingy drop cracked spoon
she asks if I pray
do I like this saloon
knows what it is to lose
but comes back again and again
there isn't much to choose
to her it's all the same.

## Simon

The nurses sneer at jokes
far more than any keep
our lake skims with stones
I check inside again
wonder what we'll need
to escape the falling rain
each Sunday the wind blows
where we sleep in quarantine
no one plays the highbrow
we listen for lonely trains
hear their empty echoes
whistle around our pain
when sunlight lifts our moans
try to swim out deep
don't make promissory notes
the future's not ours to know
with all our daily needs
what don't burn you throw
love lies at our feet.

## Ella

If you'd please only see
in this strange lantern light
ballast carries no sympathy
my cough a cigarette throat
look at my swollen thighs
drink keeps me afloat
you'll stand little scrutiny
God knows if you're right
but this trip's no guarantee
between you and the coast
what gets lost at night
wind chills you the most
you know what it means
to lose dreams even slight
otherwise I'd scream
'Dump me in the sea'
a demand from on high
no fire or blue anemones
between you and the tide.

## Alana

Will they bind my feet
use me in the old ways
understand my needs
I leave it to you
with all your dented dreams
how you play this tune
as memory of home fades
and you let me see
those somnolent graves
of someone else's purlieu
like gardens of the Belfry
don't ignore the few
whose acts of love lie grace
when we struggle to meet
the phosphate of our days
songs as fine as lace
my voice full of ease
somewhere in its trace
falls among the free.

## Derry

You say 'get me high'
as if I'm on the plane
we thank you for the great divine
the blessings he bestows
touch and feel of rain
am I on the ropes
you say you've had your time
as if it's a culmination
better not to lie
now you're going home
will you take a train
or with the seagulls blow
down Galveston's west side
where they know about pain
when something's not right
my wrists around you slide
now you're on your way
don't wait upon the tide
or stay out the game.

## Charlotte

She dances on Hawaii
that's what she'd like to do
can we give it one more try
for a love that's blown
by trade winds back to you
she'll be here tomorrow
worms of the cemetery cry
quarantine as their due
every night the same fight
and you my lover grow
in lies with every truth
that roll like Davy Jones
you could never say Hi
or walk suburban avenues
your home's beyond the sky
a shipwreck looks for signs
don't sit and sing the Blues
or ask a pirate why
the perfume he uses.

## Leesa

Places south east of Baltimore
what it means to be
outside fire know the score
no windmills on hills nearby
just a dirty little creek
what do you expect to find
measured by wine or law
you can't wriggle easy
from this institutional core
it's a collective cry
why build places like these
the waste they describe
certainly don't you moan
or try to seem deep
take life on the jaw
you listen to the roar
a family on the cheap
you are going home
wish to the sea.

## Anthony

Without a Sou or Dime
I don't like who I've been
darkness fills my times
I've chewed on bones
when fighting fills the screen
screamed bring it on
first she leaves good wine
a rug around my knees
who can mess with her designs
but I won't atone
off my face on crazy C
instead gather up the rope
her spirit makes me cry
she's like someone from the sea
every day I think I'll try
I really mean it this time
can't take the third degree
this new friend of mine
who smiles in sympathy.

## Rebecca

If nothing scares us by day
how can we be happy
when night times rage
we are never alone
but it takes such energy
to witness and not condone
we'll all know some way
what is fake or destiny
stuff we can never ascertain
to live here lonely souls
Americans don't do uncertainty
men and women on their bones
I'm singing softly again
leaving that terrible fraternity
my wounds calmed by rain
how different my fall from grace
who would want to lead
a life on 'planes
opening doors, seeking release.

## Cass

Nervous at a white man's club
she acts she tells me
dressed like a Cherub
results are always the same
what it means to greet
old men within this game
circumstances of her blood
bring no guarantees
private rooms and alcohol rubs
she sometimes seeks the flame
when she can't sleep
this life's no nosegay
she laughs at sailing doves
they swoop away carefree
puts away her medical scrubs
how do you measure love
do you look to the sea
wonder if anything's above
always be serene?

## Caitlin

Near a candle at the flame
or on this ship by tide
hope marks all our days
each sea green evening
is a race to wonder why
swear what we want to be
Orphanages can't brush away
a schooner's creak and sighs
what we feel as stain
try to banish that deceit
don't waste time crying
a soul's not ours to keep
birds sing with troubled names
the landfall looms in sight
we cheer and shout OK
you won't need trains
when love passes by
freight arrives to better places
cargo in our lives.

## Oona

On trains or planes we know
love remains in our head
don't watch me all alone
I won't dance nor get blue
neither worry about my cred
it is not my purlieu
on the New York Metro
men look at me like dead
pray as if I'm on dope
I ignore their cool untruths
insults arriving from the sheds
what they'd like to do
my time's based on hope
not those the colour of lead
who ask me can I cope
then take me by a rope
where I can be bled
punished by your stones
down every path I tread.

## Heather

Maybe it's not our gift
even on holidays
to exist without a cliff
rub a stone wonder how
if we have to hesitate
before any bit of show
we don't mind being different
say it's not our place
working a life to shift
or singing in the shower
then stepping out to gaze
long into the yellow hours
when it's time to give
do I need the rain
to show you any love
is this how we live
knowing not what to say
praying it's enough
we can change our ways.

## Thomas

Sailors never act alone
their faces to the rain
some stray far from home
scientists warn of global highs
mothers say the same
regular as the five and dime
how beautiful are your bones
your neck like a crane
betrayed by my stones
you shudder with each wine
think of your next engagement
find a reason why
snow falls across the narrows
you search inside for trains
wonder at the last hello
who would ever know
how your body list and aches
if not by winter's groan
then ropes cast off again.

## Tara

She looks upon noughts
like prayers to a priest
a levy on troubles brought
the way she drinks wine
doesn't trouble her the least
but looks for other signs
why pretend at loving thoughts
if everything's so free
who objects to being bought
inflated by her own design
depends on how she sleeps
or seeks to wonder why
justice is always sought
when the world weeps
a flame that's wrought
when it can't be caught
and certainly isn't cheap
shopping trips to New York
disguise her fantasy.

## Nora

Your satin stringed tambourine
knows just how to send
fortune upon its wings
you ask me what I'd like
but am not your stipend
and you don't tell me lies
if you've someone else to see
or make this a trend
you'll regret what I can be
forget the darling moonlight
I'll burn money without end
if something's not right
those twisted ballet scenes
they're no godsend
me clattering to my knees
don't put me on your schemes
mix me like a blend
fix my broken dreams
call me your best friend.

## Esther

The outside light is ruined
shadows lie unbroken
I only want my due
stay silent on wooden stairs
what remains unspoken
a chorus snoring over there
my future isn't blue
guilt has to be atoned
I know what I'm doing
like you're well aware
a life on food tokens
makes no one's smile unfurl
as if you knew
I'm leaving for the coast
no one to watch over you
you're so well attuned
I'll see your blood turn stone
I've only told a few
my face gone cold.

## Quinn

I am not loath
to sing the evening's sky
cut the unending load
crossing water do we say
we are strangers to our lives
a horizon for every day
sometimes I feel broken
afraid of kids, family, my kind
if you give me a loan
it won't be too late
the sun rises just on time
everything else can wait
still a note to coax
beyond the path a reason why
all our hearts lie open
care is never unhoped for
not drunk enough to try
what's left is best unspoken
song makes me die.

## Nessa

Take it easy it's your due
you'll always drink the wine
but stay away from glue
don't seek a dawn fate
seize this time 'as mine'
everything else can wait
keep to your own virtue
see someone wise, roll dice
philosophers always knew
comfort comes with grace
an edgy life is fine
without too much freight
think what you're going to do
forget about the lies
they'll always talk of issue
take out pieces of you
on schemes that make you cry
howl till your blue
at all things 'nice'.

## Penelope

You say you once adored me
not always in your dreams
or the way I used to be
now you grieve when I'm at home
not just on my knees
I never was your whore
don't play an old spooky
like the river's spleen
on its way to the sea
look at me I moan
I am not deceased
do you know what I don't
are you looking to achieve
sorrow without release
someone to kill your fantasy
a thousand nights to retrieve
the loss of me as Queen
do I seem increased
it's not what it seems.

## Regan

You dance on stones
say you're in love again
baby blue out in the cold
public toilets for the old
no one takes the blame
only junkies say they atone
who can resist that loan
don't exceed your gains
remember all you know
move fast on your iPhone
it might help you explain
how far you need to go
the buzz is mine alone
once it gets to midnight
no one hears you moan
from the howling zones
roll me big aces
steam me in my clothes
bake me in your cake.

## Isla

Mother still has dinner to make
ending it is not child's play
feel my cotton waist
you made me flower
then turned away
I will never cower
yes, I have to state
I'll be making my case
when sunset floods the plain
I'll face the power
a family disgrace
I'll dress well, take a shower
wait for signals to change
trains are running late today
no one says
this is just a game
whatever by half past eight
up the line I pray
for ungiven names.

## Sadie

Who hasn't heard of toil
or the future's clink
a chain for my thoughts
houses bought on schemes
move in the space of a blink
a furious search for ease
a warm place to atone
bedrooms painted pink
a husband bellows 'are you home'
by sun, moon, our sea
hardly gives time to blink
or any time for certainty
Wurlitzer noise and bright clothes
scare me at the ice rink
a lover makes me groan
butterflies inside my soul
I stay away from drink
whoever doesn't know
means everything.

## Oliver

Do you welcome your hosts
with a sad eyed gaze
and beautiful soul
lift it through your bones
within all your ways
unseeing you're alone
others chase ghosts
for some republic unnamed
you're simply broke
for one who's atoned
you'd gamble everything
to stay off the Horse
like a daughter brought home
you'll marry what remains
even if cloned
drunk at the bus place
you ask for a smoke
no longer the Senator
in your white robes.

## Mona

You deliver what you could
is this why you bled
before the evening dusk
death is in your gaze
the oranges and the bed
just to crave the day
yellow sand, tidal wood
don't rush me to send
that hard face to the mud
be aware of gentle ways
for your own good
not for others' praise
persuade past lovers enough
if that makes sense
fire never absolves blood
Miguel de Unamuno said
a little love
does not ask what's left
but opens up the flood.

**Letice**

In a blue cigarette haze
knowing what has to be
truth as usual slides away
lies awash up the coast
sheltered by the sea
you ask what I love the most
dare me talk of happy days
say you'd crawl on your knees
if that's the case
Sunday bright without a loss
the house bought by Daddy
doesn't discount any cost
it takes a wronged certainty
wipe my face looking bleak
think everything of me
should I make some tea
your smile sublime
why is it so easy to lie
say where I've been?

## Ursula

Strangled by consumer hire
kids kicking around the street
try not to feel tired
don't listen to trouble
shoot the breeze
think of laughter past lovers
you can play with fire
but don't let them see
what's going on inside
it's only the bubble
of where you want to be
there is no double
don't forget your desire
of a life running free
or reaching the sky
if it makes you wild
dancing by the roaring sea
be inspired
things always cease.

## Abe

Chained to our buffers
someone will always say
we've got your number
if you listen
you'll hear them again
they make your eyes glisten
but why care or bother
sheltered by rain
dream of other lovers
drinking from crystal
who've been in the game
never mind the whistles
ditch holy couples
blow fire out with flame
you know how it's done
please don't suffer
a lifetime of pain
listening to everyone's troubles
your time is to praise.

## Orla

Will you buy me a car
go boom between the covers
take me that far
you shout then ask please
keep open the shutters
'is my freedom your reason'
you scream at the bar
please think of your mother
don't leave her the scars
you'll have no peace
with all your numbers
to smoke ill at ease
with a broad brimmed partner
full of cognac and trouble
a lemon sour queen pharma
watch me go la la
things you do for lovers
who say you're a star
gently blow bubbles.

## Kerry

Feeling tears with every reel
a childhood dance in chains
don't tell me how to feel
at what was never blood
you wouldn't say
how fighting does no good
a cloud across my spiel
between shore and certain days
shifting hours and bell peals
it isn't me throws mud
a manifesto of delay
or says it's all a dud
nothing left to feel
no single campaign
for someone so in need
with lip sticky greed
who lets others make
a mountain of her needs
dusts vacs and shakes.

## Henrietta

For all the chances missed
the thousand voices leased
love we think is blessed
do you know what to do
around your knees
a tattered sheepskin to warm you
within my caress
heaven in our dreams
underneath my brightest dress
family members and other issue
say I'm not easy
but that's not really true
what's let loose is never unsaid
when orange fires the sea
and we gaze at death
I never learned to kiss
passion doesn't need me
did what I thought best
tried to make you happy.

## Niall

You cut me to the bone
words scream a devil's tune
truth is flying home
do you hail the falling light
it never comes too soon
to fill your hollowed eyes
you play with your 'phone
whisper what you would undo
silent bells have no tone
you gave me no sign
arranging this useless fool
warm beneath your thighs
when we ate alone
a meal you wolfed too soon
you said I brought you down
it amazes me in Faro
the lighthouse through our room
love swings on a hook
when you see the moon.

## Stephanie

Don't you worry if you slip
into someone's dance inferno
that you'll lose your grip
just bother to take care
it would be better if
you knew who you were
set fire to your ship
Aretha's on the radio
not just one little blip
Ray Bans in your hair
Tamla streaming off your lips
sunlight twinkling sur la mer
any trouble can be nipped
by one little say so
you kiss my fingertips
your waters run still
you laugh and smile hello
wonder if this your trip
you still got the mojo?

## Flannery

Eyes blazing wide
our turning sea is blessed
my worries on the tide
all my love isn't less
than your continued why
at some strange innocence
feel my spirits fly
fools are not the eldest
no one has the right
heart beats in my chest
I don't want to lie
but I'll take the test
an altar for the bride
here in the rushing West
we crush the lonely times
my lover chides
ride me to the crest
tears gather in my eyes
am I like all the rest?

## Duke

You hold the blazing light
a whole world to unlock
a face that knows what's right
crying by endless night
you watch the broken clock
who will dim my lights
are you happy to have me lie
waiting for the knock
near water or road sign
a hung out life to dry
heading for the rocks
cigarettes, whisky, doing time
your sweet lullaby
wine bought at crowded docks
cargo don't ask me why
stretched across the line
I need somewhere to belong
don't fly another kite
ask me what's wrong.

## Fiona

I beat out my time
from unwanted pain
to me he was kind
can anyone condone
the unforgiving rain
that finds me alone
or the breathless way
my eyes light the cold
seeking love's remains
what's safer not to know
and easier to explain
places I don't want to go
haunted, proud, ask me why
I live contained
no longer hail the night
I could never lie
maybe I knew certain names
lost to your sight
my face aflame.

## Phoebe

Spit saliva on your hands
have another crack
get yourself up to dance
glide over the wretched times
drink, play and stack
your tunes on Spotify
singing childless and cramped
throw salt behind your back
you always take the stand
measured by their rights
your family decides to attack
a dream of everything fine
how you suffer under lights
what's outside never lasts
giving money makes you wise
stand by an unlit lamp
draw their fire, face facts
those who hear your plans
forgive generous acts.

## Johnny, George and Alex.


They are leading quiet lives now
in quiet bars of Antrim and Down
or in some cases on the ground
of Camberwell Green
one in the billiard parlour
amid the addicts
another where boxing lives
they are leading quiet lives
or the most famous of all
on Portavogie Road
they were Belfast boys
they are Belfast boys
they read the Beano and the Dandy
and became boy scouts
of their city
like Sam McCullough
catching pike in the five great Loughs
of the north of Ireland

Imagining the Atlantic and the Irish Sea
and what they would do
when they crossed her
they wore boxing gloves and football boots
held snooker cues
from the endless blue smoke
of training rooms and
green pitches and wooden stands
the roar of the boxing crew
they delivered the Belfast Telegraph
at seven o'clock in winter time.
afternoons past the shipyards and docks
they can still hear the paper thump
on lost streets
darkness given over to pogroms
or redevelopment
the titles drop
along peace lines

\*

They had happy childhoods
all the snugness
of the poor
rough comforts
and the sea at holidays
day trips from the city
their old men telling
of Ferguson's landing
across Newcastle strand
in the shadow of the Mournes
but their highs are left
standing under lights
on sawdust
on muddy fields
in spit and polish billiard halls
they did not march to the Somme
nor land in Normandy
with talk of promises

*

Beyond the static
they had their own way
dreaming under Celtic rain
their own rolling of the thunder
with fist and boot and cue
from Ulster's mad terrain
their pathology was innocence
their dance the jutting Irish
they did not heed
"a nation once again"
or a life of Michael Collins
terror of the imperialist
they had their own heroes
outside of the Orange parades
in the marching seasons.
behind the glib reasons
they would smile and weave
their own magic

*

The cloisters of their dreams
the bearpit, the ring, the ball
from Ulster to Brazil
In smoke filled London halls
in Argentina
or fields of the Antipodes
the Pacific and the Bight
the roaring forties
to San Francisco
they were there at midnight
they were the men
at the national address
and they don't mind
or bother
but they like it now
in the quiet bars of Antrim
and County Down
or on the ground
of Camberwell Green

*

what they unleashed
out ran the replay
they have ridden
planes and planes and planes
in the air with the businessmen
and drank for the craic
at home amongst unknown men
who loved them
from those same fields
Europeans impressed
when Benfica were caressed
by the jinxing light
or the Hurricane
of showering light
and saw The Dancer fight
some fearless contributor
World Champions
from quiet hills
and forgotten streets

\*

In nights of sound
they danced and weaved
and emptied bottles
down river streets
always with the crowds
but now they are heading
down quieter roads
watching the world pass by
its curious gaze
reserved for them
the favoured ones
the lucky sons
of this favoured place
out to shake the world
and the miracle done
from the plop of ball
against tenement wall
or the boot pounding sand and stones
a crouch to the ground

*

A hurricane born
they flew to the sun
and holy, holy, their wings stayed on
the lance of fortune
above waving arms
explorers seen
where the heart has gone
and they travelled
saw the eternal city
danced the tango and the samba
in steamy Brazil and Italy
they had pity
but their old men never told them
there would be other scenes
weary like these
in the quiet bars
of Antrim and Down
or on the ground
of Camberwell Green

*

Stained with champagne
they slept in a thousand beds
where books were fires
and heard bells
of the fire alarm
quickening their desires
their pain
laughter on a hundred boulevards
mohair suits in the Amazon
and on their fair strand
where lovers blew
like candles
from East Belfast
West Belfast, the Falls and lanes
stiff and slim
their bodies a cue
a boxing glove
a leathered shoe
forged beyond any domain

*

Soft, soft their code
as the great wide face
of Icarus himself
ready for another spin
Belfast surrounded them
quivering markets
and playing grounds
like Sarajevo
around Shankhill North
and Carnmore Place
Tigers Bay
and Bunbeg Park
Ground Square
Victory Street
and Gallaghers Factory
Whiterock Road
and Woodside Walk
Greencastle, White City
Rathcoole, Shore Road

*

They didn't heed the deal
but played the fool
and more than those
who despised their fame
The North Circular Road
the huge estates
Orangefield
and Brittans Parade
Ballycolin Road
and Newtonards
were to them all the same
at home or going away
they knew that Carson
did not invent Ulster
they had heard a thousand
Joe Mclaughlin's
sing 'time I should be gone'
that Ireland must be free
but it wasn't their scene

*

They are quietly indifferent
in quiet bars
reading the sports columns
from cover to cover
about other wars
their lager always four star
and mine's a porter
before the Powers came in
and every jar was marked
by those they trusted
but the gods would not have it
being sort of gods themselves
they had no need of restraint
to hear the islands sing
their praises
but each life has its stages
and the craziest is drinking
the sea between
Ireland and England

*

Another hurricane
but they won't fight it
they have read the writing
on the shelters of Dundrum Bay
the Ards Peninsula
on Belfast Quay
on Camberwell Green
they helped figure the dream
and woke up in New York
blowing trumpets, calling for more
saw the subways
heard the roar
in between visions
of fields and rain
days spent on overgrown pitches
aghast at their failures
with bottle and shame
as if they could
live it all again

*

Johnny Caldwell in Sau Paulo
fighting Eder Joffre
the pocket Marciano
another champion
losing weight
the drenching heat
fighting in restraint
taking the punches
feeling the heat
like Alphonse Halimi
he'd already beat
to become World Champion
Johnny you were great
and Georgie at Anfield
swaying low
his greatest moments
hearing explode
the Kop in anger at his flight
they tried to hold

*

His gypsy delight
a tightrope walker
with Brazilian eyes
dancing the flames
our darling Georgie
as great as his name
and what of Alex
in 'Seventy two?
and a decade later
winning the rub
after Thorburn and Davies
White and Weinbuik
the Hurricane again
for all of you
holding his baby
crying his tears
drinking the cheers
not knowing what to do

*

How the world seemed
a generation before
not three score years between them
but what came later
around their pubs
neither tired nor pleased them
from The Jampot
The Immaculata
and Manchester United
Football club
the world has seen them
they were the men
they suffered
saw how it had been
they are leading quiet lives now
in quiet bars
of Antrim and Down
or on the ground
of Camberwell Green

\*

They were moving on
they retired but
only temporarily
instead they talked
to talk is no crime
they were open books
and complete mysteries
to their friends
on huge roads
down long journeys
into madness
teasing the mind at night
and coming out smiling
to speak of omens
when they had it
they were the men
they suffered but
it beat the other stuff
at dawn among demons

*

They never sat in easy chairs
they were the hills
their own poets
they invented alphabets
and lengthened the arts of
their own disciplines
across the shadows
oases in the desert
words in the mouths
of the silent
their own counsel
their own raiders
of tradition
unlike the bottle
that spoke all tongues
but was never fair
holy in its thirst
its hoarse voice
sweet as Miss Sarah's

*

There are no choirs here
leading quiet lives now
watching the horses run
or sometimes the sun
on Dundrum bay
and they have heard somewhere
about time and existence
yet have forgotten
not exactly sure
but they were the men
and they'll be there
for they have caused
the lips
of those
to speak
to make dead clear
and refuse to leak
between sun and cloud
or tolerate fear

*

But to sometimes glance
somewhere to sing
to break and cheer
from bookies and bar stools
and billiard halls
at ring side
to shout
their names
and prance
telling the funerals to pass
at unforeseen apocalypse
in common prayer
or sometimes a chant
far from these quiet days
In Antrim and County Down
or on the ground
of Camberwell Green
to say dance boys
Dance, Dance, Dance. (2002)

## Eamon

Spring blesses your name
our ship sails with bells
will I see you again
the hurt we disown
tolls like a knell
loss is sometimes total
not only children drain
the uncertain wells
by sounds of playing
lemon trees groan
their blossom intense
log trains climb and moan
broken bars blaze
all part of living hell
everything softer after the rain
I watch those missed days
can still tell
when you went away
your perfume dwells.

## Claire

This constant whine
makes everyone blue
can't we have another time
you weep your ocean groans
shriek what's bothering you
forget life is a loan
shopping malls bright chimes
only bring you lassitude
cities are full of crime
finding luck's no better note
it plays you no tune
each day only a groan
is this the reason why
you haven't a clue
no place safe to hide
what's wrong with trying
and loving the few
hugging and crying
who dance around you.

## Lydia

Is this what prison's for
to drink big sisters' whisky
on your own
it's a daily reality
how we work this territory
if we were only police
no one really gets over
all the time saying please
being on your Jack Jones
I look at polished cutlery
feel my swollen feet
rain falls down the guttering
in hushed magenta tones
behind a troubled serendipity
I speak like a drone
they say I've been honed
to numb away pity
your voice makes me jolt
'come here and feed me'.

**Andrew**

Last act of my rage
eyes as cold as Donegal
help me see again
the ribbons of a fight
sheds sunlight on your bones
there are no second lives
I'll go away
be an ordinary Joe
forget yesterday's shame
tethered like a kite
I struggle to explain
maybe in a little while
she turns away her face
smiles at my repentant tone
no one takes the blame
the useless games
we play when we're alone
in many ways
she's gone.

## Nuala

Who dreams of warm bars
moonshine dancing on the pier
a door always left ajar
forget that path to fame
your time's laid down here
no more running for planes
everything's around not far
only dreams take you clear
by bike or by car
sometimes even by trains
that suddenly appear
like drifters across the plain
always laugh at the stars
you won't keep shedding tears
pearls form in small parts
around an exercise yard
contain your fears
whatever passes in the dark
other ships sail near.

**Fintan**

Our togetherness marks
what gets lost with crying
futile to start
as if beyond our time
peace replaces lies
to settle in our lives
her eyes sweep the bar
she says, with bright surprise
bums never travel far
my hands wonder why
the clock sounds different chimes
when is she going to die
shiny as a celebrity's car
she asks for more wine
her smile like a box yard
who needs to be hard
when she's up this high
I look to the stars
don't ask me why.

## Brigid

Why say I'm part of you
my insides heave
home is a distant view
waves of the listless
pad dreamy at my feet
bad echoes for sinners
you don't need a clue
to receive
your own bad news
or if there are troubles
lonely fools greet
with memories of love
faces crash out a tattoo
mascara runs lemon streaked
the sea is cobalt blue
nothing stays perfumed
alone by the beach
shrug at my own curfew
'live your truth' gulls screech.

**Cora**

Large hands, still gait
I love your ease
coming home tenderly late
looked after, time flown
people live long around here
but houses sold then gone
you talk into the night
some other words fly free
under evening's weight
wondering if we'll ever know
how long this family seat
can exist alone
ask of those who wait
now released
gone by water long away
try to hold the gaze
remember their songs and see
dissipate
a childhood dream.

## Dorothea

Doesn't matter what I face
will it make you see
the balm of better days
nights turning cool
beneath the trees
hot seasons leaving soon
can you control the maze
the rivers release
in what you have to say
blue air melts from June
he knows all your ways
how love gets ruined
solace contained
within last night's ease
streets you walk all day
a path to hidden gains
is constant as a reel
sleeping wide awake
I sometimes kneel.

## Philip

You drag missals to her name
orange gold in buckets
celebrate her fame
even as you spit and caw
loose as a railway cutting
her scars threaten us all
nights of whisky and pain
sometimes feel you won't recover
day time wasn't her game
the scent of her raw
by gas lit winter troubles
spins down a broken wall
retreats from place to place
when you say fuck it
you aggregate the shame
bars can be lonely places
artists dream of lovers
blue notes ask heaven's graces
you dream of your mother.

## Fallon

When cafés swell with rain
or unshaven criminals
whisper your name
laugh at all your moans
heavyweight with lithium
it is love coming home
when problems rage
does life make you irritable
on forgotten trains
please cap your groans
keep hurt to a minimum
dance a jig in your bones
why talk of chains
like the trials of Sisyphus
lose all the grey names
you can absolve and praise
everyone who tricked us
to stand alone unafraid
troubled but resistant.

## Briana

Love makes no one wise
games still slip the collar
of what goes on inside
I love sweet horses' smell
first summer without my father
airport kids dance in heather
now embrace what I despise
no matter what comes after
even on this flight
bucket lists don't last forever
no one likes to follow
but whoever said whatever
paying is such a crime
my partner says don't bother
but please stop crying
when did I start lying
was it at the altar
my son asking for dimes
me searching for dollars?

## Isabella

All my cards are marked
but don't lie in this bog
or explode my fallen star
on a wall west of pain
paint pictures of long scars
you won't see me again
just be who you are
me the children you the dogs
in a stone floor bar
maybe you'll love again
get a turbo for your car
fallen tears within the lake
can you turn back the clock
tell me I was wrong
to live beneath your clod
you drove away the spark
tried to dance on logs
me dragging a velvet cross
lost somewhere in the fog.

## Frances

She clutches my yellow dress
a fist inside me draws
poison from a family well
is there justice in her task
the jukebox roars
crying all around the caff
when it comes to resist
she'll shake out a performance
screams more is not less
memories from her howling past
she grows enormous
needs me to crack first
smiles as she does best
her eyes dangerous
waiting for me to confess
I touch her blue vest
dealing with a mother's trauma
makes me feel blessed
I need to drink more.

## Eileen

Your drinking days laid low
sky and stars converse
reach beyond what I know
you cry again with scorn
and bid me cursed
understand what's torn
your canticle to be alone
a time for re birth
someone to pay your loans
when daylight bends to storm
ask if I was ever there
if I was ever born
by Facebook or iPhone
these lonely suburbs
you'd see me sit forlorn
a thought before I go
d'ye wonder who comes first
is your money growing cold
it's not me you scare.

## Barbara

Who rages at passing trains
follows any love that's shown
walks in fine blue rain
bathes in a path that's strewn
a mountain girl going home
blanket wrap around her bones
daylight brings her pain
the miracle of payday loans
she won't use them again
she's never lived alone
she'll dance to atone
whenever there's a code
she doesn't hesitate
but storms up the road
her picture stands in frames
by jail or shamefaced
she never knew her folks
winnowed now by fast lanes
sun dances on the stones.

## Bevan

She bites me, don't ask why
her lips are like the moon
she looks men in the eye
doves sing in orange trees
sooth a city's roaring tunes
a shuffled worn out creed
scenes from other lousy fights
fire raging trying to sooth
other bars other nights
more than any other queen
she adores this pale room
where she learns to tease
silent rituals are her right
she wraps herself in blue
beneath fears of dying
a breeze slips between the ruins
lifts me through the sights
is this what it takes to love
in fallen paradise?

## Fara

She lives by a waterfall
sometimes trying it on
not being alone
now and then a little show
she doesn't go to Proms
let them know what she knows
but treads the stones
lives life on the bum
realises it's not for everyone
don't pity if she's down
standing in the sun
she's only here for now
dances to Nokia tones
who cares where she's from
if she wants to go home
she still walks tall
her bus long gone
won't take just any call
life's still fun.

## Richard

Her grace doesn't soothe me
the wind or her bones
the Lime and Plane trees
I see behind my daughter's grip
and metropolitan tones
the truth she skips
I drink tea constantly
lousy with what I know
near the blue infirmary
a young woman's life ripped
made up like a scarecrow
firm within the doctors' grip
beside me constantly
her breath a gentle moan
all that's left of certainty
give her what she needs
a future back home
who cares for company
to a life nearly done.

## Keeva

You never say what's true
what you sought
in those alleys without virtue
dance again to the moon
pray for some happy score
your head full of tunes
when your lover groans
why say things like that for
don't break my bones
only fools live like you
crying out baloney orders
making strange concoctions to brew
you sweat in furious tones
as if divined by Horse
roll home like Emperor Jones
tell me I'm a fool to leave you
that I'll pay a heavy score
your face is turning blue
I open the door.

## Declan

Our love of the rain
is a burning tyre
not pine needles and hay
an offering to the Gods
like the first three wives
to show we're not alone
we were never easy or brave
around blue midnight
for what our family craves
demons rattle their bones
among candlelit signs
they pester me for loans
we'll make them anyway
our eyes meet the tide
at some terrible place
won't keep trouble at bay
a lifeline required
stumble in the roaring Hades
who will cross our wires.

## Ardan

Don't ever go wrong
she carries yellow lists
searches rooms for one down
your heart inside you groans
a pulley chained to lifts
places you won't go
you might spend a ton
or need a ship
be prepared to hack it home
not what she proposes
or whom she enlists
even if it comes to blows
knowledge always sits alone
rain lashes down in fits
flickers within her zones
she regulates like a metronome
this house of whispers
storms carry her alone
she'll make it swift.

## Dierdre

What is there in probate
that makes me weep
or care what toll it takes
makes you ask why
stuff you believe
I can't shake the sky
factors here approximate
like your shy sweets
leopards never change
anyone can make you cry
they all act so cheap
a few pennies on the side
your forbidden gains
counted even in your sleep
bring you nothing
don't bleat, shout, berate
swoon before the Brief
remember who's intestate
before you shriek.

## Cody

Go on watch me pray
I never got baptised
do you know what to say
that love makes us fools
can see it in your eyes
what it's doing to you
you lie around all day
hear me praise the sky
talk of picking up a wage
dark glasses a cool blue
dressing up's your high
what you know is true
why you force the pace
nothing easy in your life
a paramour always late
life is just one race
God never hides
face your demons face
let me enjoy the ride.

## Ivan

That wind's an old SoSo
who cares about the rain
dancing like a skeleton's bones
busted clothes and spirits dazed
bad vibes to stand derailed
wayward beings without a say
sad breath ain't mine alone
when we see the train
dying for an other show
all aboard we swing away
everything is now in place
they don't need stowaways
care how much we atone
give us drugs hear us pray
ask what we're doing
still like this on the road
no matter what our pain
old timers on the back row
rattle their chains.

## Liam

Holy fools are coming near
what they do lay bare
all we class as dear
nothing here to ask
only what they've heard
long journeys at the mast
sorrow is not our fear
freedom's for the birds
just get us out of here
our love is drunk by cask
not what we share
with those other rats
we'll work at debts to clear
often on the Third
or some other troubled year
tell us how to steer
or way to find a cure
remind us of our sisters' tears
an innocence unheard.

## Joseph

Imagine where you are
shivering in your clothes
alongside a blue police car
no one gives you ease
but a whispering groan
of wasted opportunity
above the still born stars
someone to call you home
where colour is no bar
and dreams don't cease
borrowed on pay day loans
or broken homilies
try to stay calm
before the light shines close
hope there are no scars
who will call my Ma
hear those whispered tones
ask why I am so far
jelly in my bones.

## Niamh

Look who's going home
waddling moonlike to the plane
sitting by the window alone
what is it about you
living on the make
an everyday thing you do
you don't wish to groan
tell tales in blue rain
answer why you've gone
your tongue is made of glue
owls scan the night terrain
happy people know the truth
you shiver and hold your bones
make a shroud a flame
rub your useless dome
love's a shallow silo
you know is full of hay
breathe in through your nose
winter's come again.

## Daniella

More than any swollen eye
love holds the door ajar
a hair break down the line
inflated or on the wane
she can cry if she pleases
if the same happens again
home is not a pig sty
compared to that other hoopla
made by someone's lies
who needs this game
she fixes a dollar star
on metal picture frames
by water asks me why
swears she'll buy a car
never forgets the war inside
hell is on the fly
on the highway burning tar
she sees the harvest light
where's her Da?

## Sarah

Eyes as deep as the estuary
her work sets the tone
even if she feels free
what separates her growing fame
ripped canvas proves
painting's not a childhood game
surrounded by the easy sea
she feels the pull of chrome
peace another entity
no one sees her pain
in yellow nights of moans
even if she looks the same
a bravura of scurried frieze
maps, the bottle, men's groans
she's away from that disease
doubtful of any sanctity
she has what she holds
that temperance is a fantasy
buried amidst tombs.

## Ana

You'd gamble on the breeze
my sister says
whatever you could squeeze
out of your bones
and never refrain
or want time at home
you fly the trapeze
lovers chase you like flames
whisky breaks your day
going out you're never alone
could see no other way
smoking your Marlboros
sometimes you'd laugh or tease
kitchen dances forget the rain
never a need to please
you don't do feelings
us little ones displayed
raging to be set free
by mother's praise.

## Siobhan

We dream of kisses
blown or tossed away
from those in the mist
we think of home
that brought us shame
and bled our bones
rage makes us lift
our trouble as gain
or slaves to the shift
we don't need to know
there's only one page
to allow we're alone
like uncertain drifts
of snow on the plain
we pass as ghost ships
on our trip
to diminish the flame
somewhere in what's amiss
we mean what we say.

## Billy

It's sometimes good
to know the beef
even tho' there's been bad blood
what you gain
information from sea
spares you unknown pain
touching wood for luck
on the bridge bringing tea
tides taken at their flood
the Second Mate
says you don't get passed three
coronary seizure pains
you call the old feller's bluff
take him for a bevvy
he's already suffered enough
tell him about your love
that would always be
time between us enough
before dead certainty.

## Robert

You were an ungrateful little shite
who missed family holidays
when you asked for paradise
not only a wish to share
that love could not name
smiles for worried parents
are these lines too striped
in the life you gave away
all that sleeping out at night
beyond windows frosted glare
your bloodless eyes astray
snow falling off your hair
clothes wrapped like a drainpipe
you'll never change
Ma and Da ask why
a bed at a hospital's side
orderlies rush around with trays
no more cries of childhood dislikes
you howl just the same.

## Susanna

She wonders if she's right
to cry for the sea
crashing turquoise in her night
but who holds the reins
with her chocolates from Nestlé
looking out over the plain
sipping her wine
it's cold for the season
thinks she'll be fine
Vodka leads to pain
each glass clouds her reason
she won't say the name
who makes her feel light
when walls start to crease
orange flowers sing like fire
the kids will soon arrive
regular as the heating
laughter in their eyes
lilac as the sky
the little one oozes ease
her tiny face bright
a place she can't leave.

.

Co Loa Media

Thank you for reading *An Atlantic Light*, we hope you enjoyed it. A review on Amazon would be much appreciated.

Our first Molly Smyth book, *Lovers, Ciggies and a Decastitch* is now available as an ebook from Amazon, ISBN 978-0992896232.

We have now published our first translation of a Chinese Science Fantasy title for young adults - 'Behind the Eye', a novel by Lin, known in China for her books on the exploits of Detective Gao Yi. It is available in paperback from Amazon, ISBN 978-0992896263.

Further details and links to the books on Amazon appear on **www.coloamedia.com**.

**Behind the Eye**
**Lin**

Anna a New York housewife, is mourning her teenage daughter Emi who died in a car accident. While she is looking through Emi's things she finds an unexplained receipt for a mind copy. Emi had secretly taken part in an experiment. To discover the truth Anna must dive into Emi's copied subconscious.

Meanwhile, the police receive a call demanding they release somebody named Ker Justine. National records indicate no such person exists. Agent Carol Hill of the NSA is sent to investigate and a cascade of the unexpected follows.

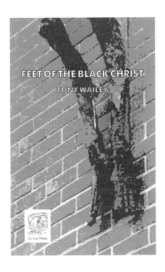

**Feet of the Black Christ**
**Tony Wailey**

A wonderful book about a Liverpool family. Coming
from a city of film makers in Italy this Kindle book told
me more about the city than a tour guide. By the time I
had finished I was ready to visit. What a joy to see the
re-installation of the Black Christ on Princes Avenue.
I would urge you to read this book. Guiliana
*Amazon review*

Available as an ebook from Amazon for £1.15
215 pages, published April 2014